HOW TO IMPROVE YOUR SIGHT

How to Improve Your Sight

Simple Daily Drills in Relaxation

By

MARGARET DARST CORBETT
(Authorized Instructor of the Bates Method)

REVISED EDITION

BONANZA BOOKS · NEW YORK

CONTENTS

HOW TO IMPROVE YOUR SIGHT

INTRODUCTION

If you have any sight at all you should develop more—not by exercise, prodding and urging tired eyes still further, but by easing and relaxing them, letting them see, ceasing to force them.

Try this. Take off your glasses and look at your watch. Not so clear? Did you have to bring it quite close? Or move it far away to tell the time? Now sit back comfortably in a chair and close your eyes. Heave a couple of deep, easy sighs. Start turning your chin from side to side as if saying slowly, "No, no," to a little child. Do not let your lids clamp shut! Everything easy—another sigh. Now look at your watch again. Any clearer? Do the eyes feel more free?

More instruction and further knowledge has frequently rejuvenated eyes and developed their power. Would you be willing to do a few simple things each day during work, during play, if it made the eyes feel rested and eased their weariness? The famous eye specialist, Doctor William H. Bates, has taught us how.

Eye sufferers who come to our studio for eye training by the Doctor Bates method repeatedly berate us for not making more public our achievements. Since our work has grown entirely by personal recommendation and without publicity, clients in many cases have learned most accidentally in a roundabout way that relief from long-standing affliction is possible.

11

"Why haven't we heard of this before?" they say. "You should let people know that permanent recovery from headache and pain and low vision is possible."

In countries across the Atlantic Ocean the Bates Method is well known and the worth of Doctor Bates' discoveries was quickly realized. In Germany the method had official recognition. His book was written for the profession, and though it gives all the necessary principles, it does not go into much detail as to their practical application to help the average man who needs relief from eye trouble. This book gives easy, simple application for the average sufferer. In other words, it tells what to do, and how, when the eyes hurt or the vision dims.

The Scientific Basis of This Book:
Dr. Bates, Our Authority

Years ago, in New York City, there lived an eye specialist of note, Doctor William H. Bates. He was an orthodox ophthalmologist, soundly scientific in all his practices and honored as an authority by other eye specialists who, when in doubt, called on him for consultation. He fitted glasses in the accepted way and operated in the important New York hospitals, enjoying an enviable practice. But for all that he was successful far beyond his colleagues, he was not satisfied.

"Why," he asked in effect, "if glasses are the correct procedure, must the glasses be strengthened because the eyes under their influence have weakened?"

Anyone who has worn glasses knows this to be the usual case. Logically, if a medicine is good the doses should be

12

weakened because the patient has grown stronger. Having an inquiring mind, Doctor Bates went into the laboratory at Columbia University and repeated the old experiments on which ophthalmology is based. He made amazing discoveries. Ancient scientists with primitive laboratory apparatus *thought* they had discovered that the lens within the eye causes refractive error. "If the lens is thick," said they, "the eye is near-sighted. If the lens is flat the eye is far-sighted. If the lens is hard the eye has old-age sight." Since they could not get at the lens, the only remedy was to place compensating glasses in front of the eye.

Doctor Bates removed the lens entirely and still found refractive error: near-sightedness, far-sightedness, astigmatism, and so on. Furthermore, he was able to train the eye to see and accommodate at different distances without the lens and without glasses. This was the most revolutionary finding. If the lens was not the cause of defective vision, what was? Again, Doctor Bates went into the laboratory. This time he discarded all book lore and former theories, and worked with eyes as he found them—as though eyes had never been studied before. He experimented on eyes of birds, fish, animals and human beings, studying inexhaustibly the action and reaction of the eye while it was used under all circumstances and conditions. He analyzed twenty thousand school children in New York City alone—happy eyes and unhappy eyes, tired eyes and rested eyes, eyes that were interested, eyes that were bored, eyes of children in a classroom they loved and in a classroom they hated. He drew revolutionary conclusions; namely, that the extrinsic muscles, not the lens, used correctly, make accommodation and, misused, cause refractive error.

These revolutionary principles have never been refuted, though in this country for purely commercial reasons they are not generally accepted. Doctor Bates himself, in pleading with the medical profession, said in effect, "If my findings are not what I say, I should be exposed and the public protected. If eyes can be normalized by simple, natural methods of relaxation, it is a breach of medical ethics not to give this boon to suffering humanity."

Elsewhere scientists accepted his principles. We understand that Germany used the Bates Method of relaxation in training the eyes of the Army, Navy, Air-force, Civil Service, and school children in *sehenschule*—"seeing schools."

It is in the hope of bringing to our public a glimpse of the Bates Method and an understanding of the wonderful relief it can bring to suffering eyes, that this book is offered.

I

HOW THE EYES SEE

The eye is like a camera. It is not the lens, Doctor Bates discovered, which enables one to see in quick accommodation, first the splinter in the finger, then the cloud over the mountain. It is the changing of the eyeball itself, the whole eyeball. The photographer changes his camera by shortening the axis for distance and lengthening it for a portrait. Just so does the eye.

We make our own refractive error or eye troubles by tightening the wrong group of muscles on the outside of the eyeball—the extrinsic muscles. When we wish to look at the mountain or the airplane in the distance we should flatten the eyeball like a lozenge, pulling the four muscles that reach from front to back: the recti. The near-sighted eye cannot do this because it is belted so tightly around the middle by the near-focusing muscles. Now when we wish to look at the splinter in the finger or read very fine print we should belt the eye around the middle by tightening the two muscles that encircle the eyeball obliquely: the obliques. The far-sighted eye cannot do this because it is already held rigidly in the flat shape of a lozenge by the far-focused muscles. Hence, refractive error is a misuse of the muscles on the exterior of the eyeball which are put there for the purpose of providing close or distant vision.

Now, all muscles can be trained; conscious muscles by direct command or exercise. But these muscles that lengthen and flatten the eyeball are not conscious muscles. It is not exercise they need. They are already held clamped too tightly. The way to train them is first to loosen them and get them relaxed. It was Doctor Bates' great discovery that when these muscles are relaxed they can be taught to function normally.

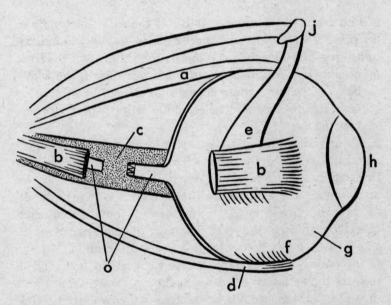

a, b, c, d are the four recti muscles, the smooth part of which flatten the eyeball; *e* and *f* are the two obliques, the smooth part of which tighten and elongate the eyeball; *o* is the optic nerve, cut to show the rectus muscle; *g* is the white of the eye to which the smooth portions of the extrinsic muscles attach; *h* is the watch crystal cornea, the window of the eye; *j* is the pulley through which the upper oblique passes.

Then refractive error should disappear. Once these extrinsic muscles are relaxed—and in the normal eye they maintain relaxation—they can be taught to lengthen and shorten the eyeball as they should. *Relaxation is the keynote of normalcy.*

Eye training and vocal training run a parallel path of procedure. The unconscious muscles of the eye and the unconscious muscles of the vocal chords must first be loosened by relaxation. Then, just as the singer with correctly placed vocal chords learns to imitate the pure tone of the trained singing voice, so the subnormal eye when relaxed and in position can be trained to imitate the activities of the normal eye.

Although all muscles can be trained, the difficulty in eye training is the fact that the smooth portions of these extrinsic muscles are not conscious muscles that can be commanded.

Anyone can speak; anyone can roll his eyes or turn them from side to side. These are conscious activities and are practiced by daily exercise of the voluntary or striped portions of the extrinsic muscles. But without training not every one can sing a clear tone. Likewise, only the perfect eye can see quickly and vividly from the close point to the distant point and back again.

Just as the voice can be taught to sing a clear tone, most eyes that can see at all can be taught to accommodate or change their shape quickly from a long axis (the close focus) to the short axis (the distant focus) and back again, registering clearer visual images on the retina. The vocal teacher instructs his voice pupil by getting his conscious throat muscles relaxed, then by helping him imitate the activities of the trained voice. The eye trainer instructs his eye student to attain normal vision by relaxing the conscious eye muscles, then by training the smooth or unconscious muscles around

17

the eyeball to imitate the normal activity of the normal eye.

There is another similarity between vocal training and eye training. Once the unconscious muscles of the vocal chords have learned to make the clear high tone, the singer can sing such tones without conscious attention, because correct habits have been thoroughly drilled into the subconscious mind. An opera singer does not have to stop and think how she should hold her throat or breathe, or shape her lips to sing a clear high C; she just does it. So it is with the eyes. Once the extrinsic muscles, the unconscious muscles on the outside of the eyeball, are trained to function normally, and drilled until correct habits are subconscious, they should act normally without conscious attention, and the more they are used the more perfect they grow.

Eyes are quick to learn, greedy to see, but rebel at strain or compulsion; once they are shown how to relax and shift seventy times per second, as does the normal eye, they adopt the habit with comfort, and like any other muscle of the body grow stronger with correct use. So, the more you use your eyes correctly the stronger they should grow, contrary to popular belief that the eye is a delicate organ which should be saved and not used very much if you wish it to last a lifetime. We all know what would happen to an arm if we saved it by carrying it in a sling to preserve it. The muscles would deteriorate; the arm would shrink in size and power. Eyes are muscles intended, like any other muscle, to be used and developed, but not misused.

Eyes are in constant motion whether one is working, sleeping or waking; whether they are used for duty or for pleasure. They might just as well be doing what you want them to do. Scientists are now investigating the relation between the continual and rhythmic motion of the heart and of the eyes. The only times eyes lose the normal seventy-times-a-second motion is when you try to hold them rigid in a stare. You are never completely successful in this. An ophthalmoscope would still show motion, but the attempted effort to slow down this movement is a great strain and injures the eye in some way. On the contrary, the moment the speed of motion is hurried, vision is improved.

II

PROTECTION AGAINST STRAIN

First, rules to protect yourself against strain in applying these relaxation drills:

One: Remove glasses before trying any of the drills in this book.

Two: Do not continue any drill to the point of weariness.

Three: Do not continue any drill until you are bored, for boredom results in eye strain.

Four: If any drill hurts or brings discomfort, stop at once; you are doing something wrong. Eyes should work without pain.

Five: Play at your relaxation drills. Do them easily; don't make work of them. They are *not* exercises. They are looseners.

Eye activity should be effortless. Vision should come to the eye as effortlessly as scent to the nostrils, music to the ear, touch of velvet to the finger tips. If in comparing several perfumes you snort and sniff violently, they soon all smell like alcohol. Effort has killed the subtle differences. If you listen "hard" to a symphony, you get the beat of percussion instruments, the sawing of violins, the blast of horns, unblended and inharmonious. If you pinch velvet or feel it violently you lose all sense of the silken pile. To get full value in the quality of perfume you must relax and let a whiff of the scent greet the nostrils. At a symphony concert you must sit back, relax and let the sounds merge and float to you in blended harmony. To sense the quality of velvet you must pass the fingers lightly over the pile, permitting the sensory nerve of touch to function unhindered by effort. So it is with vision.

Tension and conscious effort interfere with any of the special senses, including vision. To relax and let them act is the secret of perfection. When we lift our eyelids, vision should take place. No effort is necessary; any effort interferes.

A Few Dont's

If you wear glasses, take them off while doing these drills and following these instructions. This method is harmless, since it is relaxation, not exercise, and relaxation is never harmful.

Don't Rub Your Eyes

The pressure of the fist or fingers, aside from the germ and soil danger, temporarily distorts the shape of the eye. If the eyes need rubbing, do it nature's way—with the lids which are shaped to the eyeball. Squeeze the lids tightly and open them wide four or five times. The effect will be that of rubbing the eyes.

Don't Go into a "Brown Study"

Don't "park" the eyes on a spot while on a mental journey elsewhere. This habit, so frequently indulged, is the worst form of staring and can easily develop several degrees of refractive error. If you wish to meditate, close the eyes or at least blink them frequently.

Don't Duck Your Head and Look Up at the World

Balance your head above your spine so it will be on its correct axis, and it will take care of itself. Then you can look down on the world and point your nose toward whatever you wish to see. To look up from under lowered brows is always a strain and accentuates any muscle imbalance the eyes may have. The *natural* focus is downward. When an Indian looked away he lifted his head and gazed from under lowered lashes; if far, far away he tilted his head far back so that the lashes shaded the eyes. Be a nature-child yourself; look past your nose at what you wish to see.

Don't Hold Your Breath While Using Your Eyes

The eyes must have oxygen. One can turn oneself temporarily blind by holding the breath long enough. Breathe often and freely; not studied, controlled, thoughtful breathing, but easy sigh breathing such as a dog enjoys when it throws itself on the floor to sleep.

In my eye-training studio I once worked with a cataract case whose vision we had improved by our method to such an extent that I called in a doctor, who worked sympathetically with us, to examine the eyes with his powerful ophthalmoscope. One eye the doctor found to be entirely cleared of cataract. The lens of the other eye was still a little too cloudy to see the retina—to get the red reflex. "Take a long breath," I said to the pupil. The doctor exclaimed aloud that that single breath had temporarily cleared the last vestige of film in the eye, so that the retina could be seen readily. Each time the pupil remembered to breathe, the remaining shreds of sediment were dissipated. Each time he held his breath, a little murk clouded the lens once more.

22

If deep breathing will do this for a seriously affected eye, one can realize how great the benefit to normal or nearly normal vision.

Don't Force Vision

This is really impossible, for the harder you look the poorer the vision. If an object is not clear, do not look harder and harder at it. Instead, close your eyes for a brief moment; loosen yourself completely; take a deep breath; then look again easily. The object will be clearer.

Don't Blink Hard When You Blink

Check your eyelid habits. Many people do not blink enough. Failure to blink the eyes stints the lubrication and the disinfecting value of the tears that the lids should spread frequently over the eyeball. When you close your eyes to think or to sleep, do you clamp the lids down tightly? *Don't do that!* The eyes are not wild animals about to escape, but gentle, tired orbs that need the curtain lowered over the vision, softly, easily, loosely—and sigh while you do it. Your lids won't loosen? Here's a suggestion—purely mental—but it works.

The Air-Cushion Close: Hold the flat palm of your hand a foot in front of your eyes. There is a cushion of air between your hand and your eyes. Bring your hand gently closer, and pretend that the soft pressure of that air lowers your lids as the hand approaches. You will not have to bring the hand all the way; the eyes catch the idea. Now, as gently, move the hand away again. The air pressure released, the lids slip open. No effort, no conscious muscle work. Practice this to teach tense lids how easily they can do their work.

Add a blinking drill. If you tend to snap your eyes shut and open them with a jerk, practice light, feathery, flickery, quick, little blinks, not evenly and systematically timed, but irregularly, as the normal eye blinks; an animal or a baby can teach you how.

Don't Be Afraid to Let the Eyes Work

Work is good for them. The normal eye is in constant motion all the time anyhow, shifting seventy times a second whether you are awake or asleep. If you are using your eyes correctly, they will strengthen as they do their duty for your work or play, just as any other muscle increases in strength with correct use. But you must use the eyes without strain and give them plenty of rest as they work.

III

RELAXING THE EYE

Relaxation brings improved vision. It is your surest way to better sight. Prove this to yourself. Remove your glasses. Sit opposite a picture or a calendar. Close your eyes; cover them gently with the soft, warm palm of your hands; do not press. Note the rest that comes from the darkness. When you look again, with a sigh, the picture or calendar should seem brighter. The retinal nerves are stimulated by rest.

Relaxation Is a Feeling

Once experienced and practiced repeatedly, it can be maintained under ordinary conditions, and regained if temporarily lost in the stress of daily living. Loosening the big muscles over which one *has* control, permits the relaxation to flow from them into the involuntary muscles that cannot be commanded. As you sit in an easy chair wishing to relax your eyes, you *can* tell your ankles to loosen, your knees to let go, the small of your back to relax, your shoulders to loosen, your elbows and hands to unstiffen, your chest muscles to relax, your neck to ease, your jaws to unclamp, your tongue to come from the roof of your mouth, your eyelids to let go. These are all conscious things that anyone can accomplish;

at least to a certain degree and after a little training.* From these loosened conscious muscles the subconscious muscles relax by imitation. Just as tension is communicable from one person to another or from one muscle to another, so is relaxation.

Catching Eye Strain from Others

One can communicate his own eye strain by staring into another person's eyes. An extreme case of this came to my attention when the wife of a blind man came for relief from muscle spasms of the eyes. She would be downtown shopping when, without warning, her eyes would be dragged up into the top of her head and seem to lock. She would have to grope for a place to sit down and rest before they would right themselves. There was nothing functionally or organically wrong with her eyes. She caught this strain from watching the blindly staring, ill-focused, unseeing eyes of the man she loved. We handled the problem by getting both her eyes and the eyes of her husband relaxed and teaching them to stay relaxed. Strange as it may seem even blind eyes are under terrific strain, often suffering pain from tension even though the optic nerve is dead.

Once a salesman who had lost his vision but continued his sales work came to me for relaxation, though he knew no

* The efficiency of the eyes is, of course, very dependent on the posture and the relaxation of the body as a whole. The eyes of persons who are habitually tense, or of those who sit or stand with back swayed and head tilted, will, of necessity, be imbalanced. For general body posture and co-ordination of body and mind I know of no system so good as the technique of balance and co-ordination developed by Mr. and Mrs. Gerald Stanley Lee of Northampton, Mass., founders of the Coordination Guild of Northampton.

recovery of sight would be possible. In facing a business prospect his poor eyes, unseeing though they were, would undergo such tension that he would feel his face contract in a snarl. He would then frantically try to smooth it out, although realizing that he must be making grimaces. His tension and discomfort often prevented him from closing his deals. We taught him how to get his spine and neck and eyes relaxed and how to keep them so even when working, and taught him how the normal eye behaves, so that his blindly staring eyes might look and feel more normal. Now he faces his prospect comfortably and few persons realize that he is entirely without vision. The eyes shine and act normally, blinking and moving as does the normal eye. This man's sales increased because his clients no longer caught his eye strain, which had formerly distracted their attention and made their own eyes hurt to such an extent that the clients wished to escape and did not even hear what he was saying.

A trained nurse, in attendance on a long-drawn-out case of invalidism, suffered with her own eyes as she caught the sick person's strain. We were able to teach her to keep her eyes relaxed, comfortable and normal even under these conditions.

An actor caught eye strain from the eyes of his tense, erratic director. In taking final directions before going in front of the cameras, he had to look into the director's eyes to show attention, and always turned away with his own eyes tight and painful and in no condition to do himself justice before the cameras. We taught him how to keep his eyes relaxed, to avoid catching the other man's strain, and his expression improved on the screen.

The Mental Side of Vision

The optic nerve actually contacts the brain to carry the message that a picture has been taken on the retina which the mind must interpret. Hence, the optic nerve is really part of the brain, and vision is *nine-tenths mental* and only one-tenth physical. You have frequently proved this to yourself in reading an uninteresting page. Your eye dutifully took in every word, but at the end of the page you knew nothing that you had read because your mind was not in attendance. Because the mind did not do its part, vision was not completed. The most important part of vision takes place in the mind. There is no such thing as eye strain without first a mental strain—a mental effort or confusion. Get rid of this mental effort or strain, and your vision will improve. Eyes are tough to what happens from the exterior. They mend readily from scratches, bumps, even burns; or learn to see around scar tissue; but eyes can be blinded from within by mental strain.

Palming

One of the most important ways to get rid of both physical and mental strain is by palming. Lay the palm of one hand along the side of the nose so that the fingers are high on the forehead and the hollow of the palm is closed over the orbit of the eye. The eye will not be pressed but will be free to blink, though the lashes may touch the palm. Now, without dislodging that hand, lay the other hand along the other side of the nose; the fingers will cross on the forehead. The heel of the hand will rest on the cheekbones. There will be a slight suction under the palm. Rest your elbows on something at a comfortable height as you sit relaxing, so that the neck is not bent forward but is on a line with the spine. The eyes will close as relaxation sets in and should remain closed, the condition of rest. This may be the only time the eyes rest, because strained eyes when you close them close tightly, and stay rigid and continue straining during sleep unless relaxed first. Physically, palming does wonders for the eyes. It speeds circulation through the eyeball to carry away impurities and to bring fresh stimulation to the retina—to the little rods and cones, the nerve ends that do our actual seeing.

If one palms mentally as well as physically, double value will be attained. Palming mentally means relaxing the mind. This seems a large order for a rushed and hurried individual, even though he has a five-minute respite during the day.

Palming

Now, the secret of mental relaxation is *memory*. Pleasant, happy memory of something you have seen and enjoyed seeing brings relaxation to the mind and eyes. Return mentally to some favorite spot—a view of the ocean, a favorite place in the mountains, a fragrant garden, a lovely drive on a winding highway; the memory will bring relaxation.

One harried business man could bring himself immediate relaxation in a five-minute palming period, wedged into a hectic office day, by taking himself back to a scene of his youth—a summer day on the Charles River. He would go again in cool boating togs to the old boat house among the willows, ease his canoe down the slide into the coaxing water, step aboard with his paddle and settle back into the upholstered seat. In memory he would dip his blade in the smooth-running stream and glide noiselessly along the shore around this familiar bend, past a beautiful estate with lawns stretching to the water's edge, past a swan posing in a cove, and along the willow-lined banks to the gay boat-club decorated for a tilting tournament. Before five minutes had passed this man's eyes were rested and his soul refreshed; not only eyes but mind had been relaxed. *Happy memory brings relaxation.*

A young mother found relaxation in reliving the thrills of her baby girl at her three-year-old birthday party. The pleasure with which she watched the shining faces around the party table, and the big eyes as the goodies were served, always brought this mother rest.

A father found ease in reliving the graduation exercises of his son, watching again in memory the long line of earnest lads in caps and gowns as they filed across the platform for the coveted sheepskin.

If your nerves are so tight that you cannot conjure up a restful picture as you palm, follow the mechanical memory drill noted below.

Mental Blackboard

Go back in memory to some blackboard you stood before as a child. Stand there again; take chalk in one hand, eraser in the other. The blackboard has been freshly washed, the blackest black, no chalk dust anywhere. On this clean blackboard print capital A. Erase it immediately, then write capital B, and rub it out, then capital C; erase—and capital D. Clean the board. Continue this unless the blackboard gets chalky. It must be kept black, so go to the window, lean out and tap the eraser against the wall on the outside, letting the breeze blow the chalk dust away. Now return and polish the blackboard until it acquires a fresh blackness and continue with your alphabet. By the time you have done the alphabet in capitals, and perhaps repeated it in small print, your eyes will be relaxed and you will feel rested in all the nerves of your body. Next time you are threatened with exhaustion and headache, *palm!*

IV

SUN AND LIGHT

Does sun bother your eyes? Do you dread driving against the glare on the highways? Does sunshine on the ocean spoil your days at the beach? Do headlights hinder your night driving? Are you annoyed by the lights in an auditorium? Would you like to be free of this pain and discomfort, able to do normal seeing in God's sunshine, free from annoyance from man's imitation of it? Then teach the eyes to "accept" the light.

Eyes are built for light. They are the one organ of the body constructed to receive and use light. Good vision takes place only in light. With the rising sun, vision improves; as twilight deepens and dark sets in, vision grows dimmer. When days are dark and cloudy, people feel low or depressed. They don't realize why, but the increased effort to see in poor daylight taxes their nerve force by demanding more effort of their eyes. This saps their vitality.

Eyes that have plenty of light are strong, but eyes that are starved for light suffer failing vision. It is so in all nature—with birds, beasts and fish. The sparrow catches his dinner in the sunbeam. Trout living in shallow water near the surface have excellent vision and leap into the light for the fly. But fish in the ocean depths, where no light penetrates, are blind. So are fish in underground rivers.

A miner in Arizona picked up a tubful of these blind fish which could not see to escape his hand. He put them in the gold-fish pool on his estate where the hot, Arizona sun shone down on the water. Weeks later he took some friends to see these curiosities in the gold-fish pool. The blind fish had regained their vision and were so observant and quick-moving that the visitors could not get within the pool's width of them.

The little burros taken to the depths of the coal mines lose their vision, but allowed a vacation frolic in the sunny fields, they, too, regain their eyesight.

With human eyes it is the same. Among coal miners eye disease and blindness are very prevalent. This is true also of shipping clerks who travel in subways and toil in sub-basements. Sea captains and sailors have excellent vision, though they are subjected to a constant, relentless glare and brilliant light both from the heavens and the surface of the water. This good eyesight is true also of desert men and primitive natives. Yet on the desert there is no shade, but unrelieved sunshine.

The popular belief that eyes should be protected from sunshine probably arose from the fact that eyes, if at all nervous or strained, resent sudden contrast, as when you step from a shaded building into the brilliance of the noonday glare. This shock tightens tense eyes to the point of pain. But it is the suddenness, not the brightness, that does the damage; the very tightening, and not the sunlight, shuts off the circulation which robs the eyes of necessary blood and oxygen; a painful condition.

Remove glasses and try the following sun drills. Ease your eyes into the brilliant light; close them and loosen your eye muscles if tense. Sit or stand with the lids closed for a moment, moving your head gently but quickly from the shade on one side through the brilliant sun into the shade on the other side. Take deep breaths as you do this. Loosen the eyelids and the face muscles. If this seems severe after a few motions, turn your back and rest. Then repeat, more loosely this time. Once the sun grows comfortable to your closed lids, the glare on the streets will not be bothersome when you open your eyes to glance in one direction then the other.

Now give your eyes a feast of light. Cover the left eye with one palm so no light can enter. Breathing deeply, swing the head and elbow and blink with the right eye several times through the sun. Surprisingly, this will not bother the eye. Then cover the right eye and repeat. It should not be long before you can blink rapidly at the sun with one eye at a time and not feel discomfort. There will be little spots or after-images of the sun following these blinkings. This is normal. Do not be alarmed, but cover the eyes with the palms and let them rest for a moment. Then dip your closed lids into the sun again. Repeated practice of this sun drill should strengthen the eyes for light to the point where no amount of glare can bother them.

Sun is three-fold in its value. It relaxes the muscles—crossed eyes are never so crooked immediately after a sun bath. It stimulates the retina—even blindish, dimming eyes have greater vision after sunning. Sun is the best remedy for granulated lids, itching or bloodshot eyes.

Give your eyes a sunning at every possible opportunity. This does not mean to stay in a blazing sun until faint or prostrated with the heat. Use judgment in the length of time you spend, in the dose you take. Do not sun until uncomfortable. The eye will stand more sun than the skin will comfortably take. Let you skin be your guide.

If you pass your daytime in an office, choose the sunny side of the street on your way to work in the morning. Save a few moments of your noon hour to sun your closed lids. Get another nip of sun as you pass a sunny window in the afternoon and at the close of day.

When motoring, bathe your eyes often in sunshine and the glare of the highway will not be annoying.

If you spend most of the day indoors have the rooms well lighted. At home many women dwell in semi-darkness. In the forenoon shades are drawn to prevent fading of upholstery and drapes. In the afternoon, bridge and tea are candle-lighted. Such eyes, starved for sunshine, flinch against the light of day. Sun baths should be given these eyes as regularly as meals are taken.

The beautifying effect of sun on eyes is miraculous. Eyes that take their sun baths have a sparkle and high luster that no beauty drops ever gave. Such eyes are never watery, gritty or bloodshot. Well-sunned eyes are wide and shining—youthful eyes.

V

SWINGING*

All our lives doctors have said, "Relax and your health and nerves will be better." They did not, however, tell us how to relax. Here are a few simple, natural methods that the most nervous persons can use with success.

The Bear Swing

We have all seen a lion or a bear at the zoo swaying rhythmically back and forth behind his bars. This is not fretfulness or desire to escape but his method of keeping relaxed. Try it yourself. Find yourself a series of bars—the ribbons on the Venetian blinds, or even one window-cord on a shade, will do. Start swaying, like the bear, from side to side, taking all of you—head, eyes and body—to one side, then all of you to the other side, in a rhythmic sway, humming a soft waltz tune as you rock from one foot to the other. The bars or ribbons will pass you, moving in the opposite direction just as they pass before the face of the bear. You will see them slipping by, but do not stop to look or they will cease to move and you will feel a slight dizziness. Let your eyes travel with your nose, looking off into the distance where your nose is pointing.

* Without glasses.

The Long Swing

Add a slight turn, at the end of the bear swing, on the right, then on the left—more like the swing of the elephant's trunk when he weaves to keep himself calm. The world will seem to revolve about you in a gentle arc, slipping by from one shoulder to the other. Let it slip by. This is the optical illusion of normal vision.

One hundred of these swings take but a few moments and accomplish wonderful things for the body. This swing is a spinal massage, coaxing the rust out of the hinges, speeding the circulation. It loosens tensions in the inner organs, often doing away with indigestion and intestinal troubles. Before bedtime it promotes restful sleep, combating insomnia. But most important of all it starts your eyes on their very essential seventy-times-a-second movements which are necessary for normal vision.

Rocking Chair Swing

It is natural to rock back and forth. Explorers report that monkey mothers rock their babies in the jungle. If modern mothers did likewise, not only the children but the mothers would be more relaxed.

Pretend that your straight chair is a rocker, unless you possess a real rocking chair. Rock way back from the waistline, letting head and eyes go far back on the ceiling; then rock way forward, until your head and eyes hang low to your knees. Do this gently and rhythmically half a dozen times, noticing that when head and eyes are rocked way back the world is below, under your chin. When you rock forward, head hanging by its roots, the world is far up over your head. You would have to raise your head and eyes to see it. Doctor Bates said, "The world moves; let it move. Never try to interfere with its movement." You and your line of vision are the center of your universe; the world passes by. To prove this illusion turn your head and sweep your vision from one corner of the room along the far wall to the other corner, and notice you have left behind not only your starting point but the whole wall, just as though it were a moving-picture-set on rollers. Practice sweeping back and forth the length of the wall until you develop the illusion of the wall sliding by. This is *not* an eye exercise but a loosener.

The Pencil Swing

Hold your pencil up five inches before your nose. Now swing the head from shoulder to shoulder letting your eyes slip along where the nose points. The pencil will seem to pass from one side of your face to the other in gentle rhythm.

It's Always Swing Time with Normal Eyes

The purposes of the swing:

One: It starts the eye shifting.

Two: It stimulates circulation in neck, eyes and spine.

Three: It sensitizes all parts of the retina, the sensitive plate in the rear of the eye, which, by giving all parts a chance at the object, takes the picture.

Four: It gives the numbed or paralyzed fovea (center of sight) an opportunity to contact the image and reawaken. This is very essential, since the strained eye tries to do its seeing with less important portions of the retina while the keenest part, the fovea, becomes numb from disuse.

VI

MENTAL DRILLS

Consider these drills a bag of tricks, held in reserve to be taken out one at a time on different occasions of need, filed away for future reference in the emergency created by tension.

Nose Writing

This may sound foolish, but its basis is scientific. It is wonderful relaxation for nerves and the muscles of eyes and neck. Flop into an easy chair or lie in bed—and I mean really loosen and flop! Lift your hands and drop them, palms up, into your lap. Unclamp your teeth; heave a sigh. Now, pretend your nose is eight inches longer than its true length. With this elongated pencil-nose we are going to draw pictures and write words. Eyes closed but not tightly!

The Wheel

Imagining the neck as a pivot on which the head moves easily, draw a large circle, the rim of a wheel, with the end of this long pencil-nose. Go over it several times, round and round, smoothing out any flat tires. Now, around the other direction just as thoughtfully. Next put spokes in your wheel all the way from the top of the wheel to the base, carefully going through the hub in the middle, up and down several times to steady these spokes. Now, sidewise spokes from side to side, then kitty-corner spokes, now catty-corner spokes. Next, draw the round hub of the wheel. Now poke in the axle hole; every wheel must have an axle hole.

The Lazy Eight

We are now going to draw a large, fat "eight" with the tip of this long nose-pencil. But instead of having the "eight" stand up, lay it on its side so that one loop is in front of one shoulder and the other loop is in front of the other shoulder. Eyes closed all the time. (*Note:* Keep the head above the spine and work gently. This is not an exercise.)

Word Writing

Now, with your nose write your own name in longhand with the free movement. Begin away at the left shoulder so as to have plenty of room. You can follow this with some "rest" words, such as comfort, leisure, happiness—anything pleasant that comes to mind.

The most important part of nose writing is the ability to test your own degree of relaxation by the perfection of the mental picture you have drawn. If the letters of your name were cramped, it is an indication that the neck or eyes are still tense. Imperfect drawing—imperfect relaxation; perfect drawing—perfect relaxation.

Scientific Basis for Nose Writing: Normal eyes and mind work in perfect co-ordination. You cannot think a mental picture without the eyes envisioning it. When you think a mental picture, the eyes at once start moving their seventy-times-a-second shift. The minute this shift is encouraged, relaxation follows and the vision becomes better. Memory relaxes—mental pictures are memory.

File Card Drills

These should be taken with the eyes closed. You will like some better than others. Call on your favorites often.

Mental Drill One: Swing the Dot

On the mental desk before you (in the mind's eye) is a package of file cards, dead-white, of lovely quality, keen edges, sharp corners. Select a card; run your fingers around the edges and across the surface, noting the quality. Now lay this mental card on your mental desk and reach for a pen. Dip the pen in a bottle of India ink, the blackest ink you can ever imagine. In the center of this file card draw a round black dot the size of a pea. Make it very round and very black; blow the ink until it is dry, then add another coating of black ink. Now lay the pen aside. Observe the white of the card a quarter of an inch to the left of the dot you have drawn, then quickly shift your attention to the white on the other side of the dot. Keep up this shift of attention rapidly and rhythmically, from white on one side of the dot to white

Mental Drill Chart Number One

42

on the other side. The dot will appear to shuttle back and forth, the opposite way from the side you are observing. Keep the dot shuttling until you tire of it, then throw the card into your mental waste basket. We can be extravagant with these cards. Take a fresh card, draw a smaller dot and shuttle. Continue until relaxed.

Mental Drill Two: Dot—Circle—Dot

Reach for another file card. Lay it on the desk before you. Dip the pen in India ink. In the upper left-hand corner draw a black dot. In the upper right-hand corner a similar one. Now, in the center of the card draw a round black O the size of a quarter. Make the O very round and very black so that the white background shines white from the middle and the file card whiteness gleams brightly around it. Lay your pen aside. Now, look at the dot in one corner, then shift across the top of the card to the dot in the other corner, back and forth, smoothly and rhythmically. The O below swings gracefully from side to side, like a pendulum, in the opposite direction from your line of vision.

Mental Drill Chart Number Two

Mental Drill Three: Semi-Colon—Colon

Help yourself to a new file card. Place it on the desk. Again dip your pen. This time draw a semi-colon and beside it, a colon. Lay pen aside. Now shift your attention from the top dot of the semi-colon across to the top dot of the colon; drop to the lower dot and back to the comma of the semi-colon and up to the original dot. This is a very restful mental picture, and can be done in public when one would like to palm but can only close the eyes.

Mental Drill Chart Number Three

44

Mental Drill Four: Dot—Line—Dot

Reach for a fresh file card. Lay it on the desk and take your pen. Divide your card in equal halves by an inch-long line in the middle. In the center of each half make a round black dot the size of a pencil end. Make the dots very black and the dividing line very firm. Lay your pen aside. Now shift your attention from the dot in one half to the dot in the other half, back and forth until the line begins to shuttle rhythmically in the opposite direction.

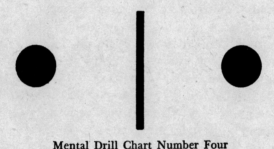

Mental Drill Chart Number Four

VII

SHIFTING*

It has been said that when the eye shifts, it sees. The shifting eye catches everything; the fixed eye sees spottily, here and there, and is startled by something that appears suddenly from the side. Staring ruins eyes. Moving or shifting is the opposite of staring, and is the beginning of better vision. Hence the first law of vision is, "When the eye shifts it sees. When the eye fixes or stares, vision fails." Do not confuse "shifting" with "shifty." The shifty or evasive eye is most undesirable and repels. The shifting eye attracts because of its fascinating, tiny, twinkling motions—the aliveness that only the normal eye possesses. This motion can be readily observed on the picture screen in close-ups of stars with normal eyes, notably the dancing, sparkling eyes of a popular skating star.

You, too, may develop these twinkling eyes and the better vision that accompanies them, in many easy ways—first of all, by the swings described in Chapter V.

Second, use your eyes as paint brushes, not as blotting paper. When you look at an object or a picture do not try to absorb it in a blotch as would a blotter, but travel all over it with your vision as though you were repainting it. You will

* Without glasses.

46

find, as this method becomes subconscious habit instead of conscious command, the eyes will travel of their own free will and your memory as well as your vision will improve. Imperfect eyes, fixed eyes, see only one part of what they look at, hence *remember* only part. When the eyes learn to shift normally, memory should improve.

Third, do you have trouble remembering faces? Do your eyes tire in social or business conversation? Check your habits when talking to people. Do you stare at them, fasten your gaze on one eye or try to fasten on both eyes? The normal way of looking at a person is to let your visual attention travel from one of his eyes to the other, from the bridge of his nose to the tip, a quick trip around his face and back to his eyes. One would think this motion would be noticeable and look peculiar. In reality, the movement takes place deep within your own eye, in the center of sight of the retina, the large muscles scarcely moving at all. It may feel as though the eyes were swinging from ear to ear but the effect on the observer is just a pleasant twinkling quiver of aliveness that compels the attention. Practice this pupil-to-pupil shift consciously on your relatives and intimates until your eyes have formed the twinkling habit and are able to do it unconsciously. Then it should not tire or strain your eyes to be with people socially or in business. Eye strain is contagious; you can hurt other people's eyes by staring at them or you can catch their eye strain if they stare at you. This conversational shift prevents strain both ways and increases your attractiveness to others.

Keeping relaxed in your dealings, whether business or social, with other humans gives you magnetism. I would almost say, *is* magnetism. You know from your own experience that you wish to escape from tense people. Even though you like them it is unpleasant to associate with them. On the other hand, persons who keep relaxed in personal contacts draw you to them. You feel easy, comfortable; you do not mind seeing them often. This also works the other way around; if you are tense you repel others. If you feel easy and relaxed, particularly if your eyes are comfortable and relaxed, you draw others like a magnet. They like to be with you. We repeat: eye strain is contagious, easily passed from one individual to another. Tension is communicable; so is relaxation. If you make the person to whom you talk sufficiently tense and strained, his mind will become so confused that he may not even hear or comprehend what you are saying. If you get him relaxed and keep him so, every word you say will be heard and will have weight.

The faster the visual shift the better the vision. Speed up your eyes.

To teach the eye to shift, develop a fast counting habit. Accustom the eye to the habit of counting series of things instead of parking statistically here or there; count the cornices on a building, the rows of windows in a passing train, blackbirds on a lawn, the folds in a curtain, the designs on a rug or wallpaper. Do not try to be accurate—just pretend to count. As time goes on, the eye will skip fewer items in the series and your count will grow more accurate of its own accord.

Take two small rubber balls; learn to juggle, being sure to keep your eyes on the ball as it leaves the right hand and lands in the left. Avoid staring into the sky and waiting for the balls. Remember the rule, "Keep your eye on the ball!"

Domino Drill

Get yourself a box of dominoes that go as high as double nines.

Step One: Pick up one domino at a time; hold it at arm's length; pass your eyes across it quickly and close them immediately. With the eyes still closed, say what you saw on the left half, on the right half. Verify; lay it aside. Take another. Passing the eyes across a domino briefly once is enough. The eyes are so quick they will catch the picture before the mind has a chance to read it. Sight is quicker than thought. Keep the lids closed to give the slower mind time to read the image photographed. As you practice this, eye-mind co-ordination will become more perfect.

Step Two: Place a layer of dominoes in the lid of the box. See how quickly you can read the upper halves of the first row of dominoes, crossing the box from left to right. Repeat with each row of halves in the tray. At first you will be able to see them quicker than you can think and say them.

Step Three: Stand a row of twelve dominoes facing you along the edge of a table. Sit in front of them, at a distance where you can read them comfortably. First, make your eyes count the twelve for speed of eye-mind shifting down the row. Then flash back to the first domino; close your lids at once and name the number on top, and the number below, of the first domino. You will have seen it. Trust your vision. Open and verify. Count the twelve quickly again; snap back to the second domino. Flash from the top down on it, and close and name. Continue until you have flashed back to each domino in the row.

See how quickly and accurately you can read the top half of each domino down the row; then the lower half. Repeat reading from the opposite direction. Speed is our objective.

Now see how quickly you can read the little top row of dots along the upper edge of the domino all the way down the twelve; now the next row, next, et cetera.

If you have trouble seeing things at a distance, you can gradually move farther back from the row of dominoes to stretch your distant vision. If your trouble is at the near point, keep moving closer.

This domino work clears up astigmatism by speeding the eyes. The entire retina jumps from domino to domino, but more important the fovea, or keenest portion of the retina, travels from dot to dot, passing over each dot no matter how fast you read. It also goes around each tiny dot, so that if one were a triangle and another a square you would notice it.

Calendar Drill

This drill builds vision and strengthens the eyes. Palm before starting and after each step of this drill.

Secure a commercial calendar that has a large month in the upper portion and two smaller calendars, the previous and following month, in the lower portion. Hang it on a wall, the height of your eyes when you are sitting opposite and with as good a light on it as possible. Place your chair at a distance to read the large numbers easily. Now palm your eyes until relaxed.

Step One: Glance over your left shoulder and sweep your head and eyes to the number one on the big calendar. Close eyes, rest and breathe. Glance over the right shoulder and

FEBRUARY						
SUN	MON	TUE	WED	THU	FRI	SAT
1	2	3	4	5	6	7
8	9	10	11	12	13	14
15	16	17	18	19	20	21
22	23	24	25	26	27	28
29						

JANUARY						
SUN	MON	TUE	WED	THU	FRI	SAT
				1	2	3
4	5	6	7	8	9	10
11	12	13	14	15	16	17
18	19	20	21	22	23	24
25	26	27	28	29	30	31

MARCH						
SUN	MON	TUE	WED	THU	FRI	SAT
	1	2	3	4	5	6
7	8	9	10	11	12	13
14	15	16	17	18	19	20
21	22	23	24	25	26	27
28	29	30	31			

slide your eyes under the row of numbers to number two. Close eyes, rest and breathe. Glance over the left shoulder and slide your eyes under the row to number three, et cetera.

Simple as this drill seems, it tricks the subnormal eye into doing all the natural things the normal eye does unconsciously. It is important to slide *under* the row of numbers each time to get to the number you want. That teaches the eye to shift, then to centralize or see the *one* number, in the midst of that conglomeration of shapes, better than all the others, i.e., Central Fixation.

Step Two: Palm and relax the eyes. This is the big shift and is a conscious motion done by the big muscles of the eyes.

Breathe deeply; open the eyes on number one of the large upper calendar, then drop to the smaller one on the left lower calendar, and close eyes. Open again on the big number one and drop to the number one on the right lower calendar. Close eyes and breathe. Continue from the big two to the left lower two and close; from the big two to the right lower two, and close, et cetera. Be sure to close eyes after every shift, as the progress comes only while you keep the eyes rested and relaxed. Do not forget to breathe deeply.

Step Three: The small shift—an unconscious motion done by the inner portion of the eye. This will seem purely a mental thing, but the center of sight actually travels. Open the eyes at the top of the large number one and shift vision and attention to the base of the number, and close. Open at the top of number two and shift to the base, and close, et cetera.

Step Four: Palm. With eyes closed give yourself a number. Open and see how quickly you can find it on the big calendar and on each of the smaller ones. You will have to do a good deal of scuttling about to find it.

If you have not time to do each step through the entire calendar, do two rows of each step rather than use all your time on the first step.

Close the eyes often. If you rest *before* you tire, you will never grow weary.

To normalize your vision, then, keep your eyes painting, shifting, counting—which relaxes them. Palm at frequent intervals for rest, and use the sun as the tonic.

As the vision improves daily and you survey the universe, you will get the effect that all the world has had its face washed.

VIII

MYOPIA—NEAR-SIGHTEDNESS

Near-sighted eyes need much done for them to bring them to normalcy. First, they must have their tension relaxed so that the oblique muscles that belt the eye too tightly about the middle will let go. Then, the recti muscles must be strengthened so that they can flatten the eyeball for the distant focus; and in addition their endurance must be built up so that they can maintain their hold on the eyeball longer than a mere second or "flash," which most near-sighted eyes can get after just a little relaxation.

Myopic eyes of many pupils get a flash—a touch of normal vision. Suddenly the oblique muscles let go and the recti contract, shaping the eyeball normally for a moment or two so that the entire panorama stands out perfectly just as with normal vision. The vision is so vivid and comes so suddenly that it literally takes the breath away, and they gasp or cry out. These flashes are sure proofs that vision is within the eye, as soon as the eye can be relaxed to permit vision to take place. Vision is like a faucet: tension turns it off, relaxation turns it on.

Furthermore, with myopic eyes not only the extrinsic muscles must be strengthened but the retina itself must be re-enlivened, since the rods and cones of the myopic retina, the nerve ends that actually do the seeing, are numb from disuse. They are accustomed to act only under the stimulation of an exaggerated image produced by strong lenses— shock vision that the strong glasses have been giving. These nerves have to be awakened to the slight image thrown on them by the unaided eye, naturally a weak picture at first. Not only must these retinal nerves be re-enlivened, but the brain cells back of the optic nerve must be aroused and taught to pay attention even to a slight picture carried to them by the optic nerve.

Naturally, this all takes time; but realize also that the eyes have been near-sighted a long time. You will be encouraged to continue by the greater distance the eyes will gain, and by the elimination of the tension in eyes, neck, back and nerves in general. Most myopic eyes can be brought to complete normalcy by relaxation, though it is hard for a person with a high degree of myopia to work without the aid of a skilled teacher, for this reason: eye strain is an unconscious strain. You do not know you are straining until after the vision is lowered and it is too late. It is a hard habit to break without help. However, until a well-trained Bates instructor can be contacted, the suggestions in this book can be used with advantage to arrest progressive myopia and strengthen the eyes. Many people who have a high degree of myopia own a box full of weaker glasses previously discarded as their eyes have required more powerful lenses. Such persons have been able, working alone, to improve their vision so that they could graduate back to weaker glasses after learning to keep their eyes relaxed. And they have enjoyed better vision, with less nervous tension, using these weaker glasses than they had had with the more powerful lenses before practicing these Bates principles.

I suggest that you do not use a letter chart in working alone. It takes all the skill of a thoroughly trained instructor to prevent near-sighted eyes from making great effort on charts. Use, instead, a calendar. Since knowledge of the sequence of numbers is almost subconscious, it is no effort. The calendar described in the chapter on shifting is excellent for this.

Remove your glasses and hang this three-part calendar in the best light you have. The numbers in the larger portion should be two inches high, in each of the lower portions, about an inch. First of all find out just how close you have to sit to the big numbers to make them out with both eyes. Make a record of this, measuring your distance, then try each eye separately, and record. Keep this record for later comparison. Prepare your eyes for your lesson by palming and sunning them or "dipping" them in the strongest light you have. Resolve to look easily and breathe deeply; carefully avoid squinting, or squeezing the lids, to clear the vision. This is trick vision and injures the eyes. We want only normalcy, no tricks. Try to keep the weight of heavy upper lids from bearing down on the top of the eyeball. Each time you breathe deeply, tell yourself to get the weight of the upper lids and brows off the eyes. Give yourself the calendar drill, formerly described, step by step, carefully for half an hour each evening if you are busy during the day. If your time is your own, plan your calendar drill when good daylight, or, better yet, *sunshine* can strike the calendar. Work first with both eyes, keeping the head in gentle motion all the time, turning the chin from side to side as if saying, "No, no," to a little child.

After a week of this, start working a little with the weaker eye, putting a patch or tying a handkerchief over the stronger eye, loosely enough so that you can blink and close and open freely.

As your vision improves you will be able to move your chair progressively farther from the calendar. Be generous with your palming; rest between each calendar step to avoid after-weariness. It is only logical that if you look easily, and rest before you are weary, you will not tire your eyes.

Near-sighted eyes can add the following step to the calendar drill. Hold your watch close enough to your nose to make out the numbers on its face with comfort. Read number one on the watch and glance at number one on the calendar, lifting your face to point your nose at it. Close your eyes, swing your head and breathe. Read number two on the watch and glance at number two on the calendar, et cetera. This simple drill jolts loose the tightened oblique muscles and tenses quickly the recti which are needed for distance.

The domino game, previously described in the chapter on shifting, can be used to increase distant vision. Start close enough to read the dominoes easily as they are lined up on the table; then move back a foot and repeat, increasing your distance from day to day as you are able.

After a couple of weeks of earnest practice of these relaxation methods and vision-stretching drills, you should be able to go about your room without your glasses with increasing comfort and vision. Soon you will be able to eat your meals without them. Give your eyes all the vacation possible from the lenses each day, a chance to act on their own at such times as you are not under stress. Do not attempt to go into traffic, or drive a car, without glasses until you can pass the drivers' tests without them, even though you might feel that you could, for the myopic eye is slow as well as short-sighted.

Motoring Drill

When you are a passenger in a streetcar, train or automobile, remove your glasses and see what large billboards and signs you can read as they flash by in transit. The speed of the vehicle, added to the increasing speed of your eyes, is a great stimulant to vision. If you pass the same route daily you will notice an improvement.

License Plate Drill

Read the first two numbers on automobile license plates of moving cars.

Motion Picture Drill

At the picture show sit in the third or fourth row. At first, take off your glasses only during a part of the show, as the eyes still lack endurance. Perhaps the picture at first seems too blurred to enjoy. Be patient for a few moments; soon the screen will start to clear, and before many trials you will be able to read the captions. Palm during the advertisements, during the "teasers," and your vision should improve even during one show. Keep your head high, looking easily at the screen; breathe often; do not let yourself tighten or make too great an effort. Before many shows you should be able to sit farther back; increase your distance as you can.

Recognition of faces is the greatest ordeal for the near-sighted eye. The reason for this is that faces are so similar, all having eyes, brows, noses, mouths and hairlines. The finer distinctions of expression are too subtle for dull retinal nerves. So, go without your glasses frequently and practice recognition of friends right from the beginning. A person should be able to recognize a friend from a side or a rear view at a reasonable distance, using the face simply for verification. But the myopic eye, the moment a human comes in sight, begins to worry about the recognition and fastens its gaze upon the face in a panicky stare the minute the face appears. By the time the person is close enough to be recognized, the near-sighted eyes have lost what vision they did have from the exhaustion of staring. The normal eye, on the other hand, seeing a person coming, sweeps from head to toe for anything that looks familiar. Then it begins to analyze the swing of the body and the walk, the angle of the head on the shoulders, the motion of the shoulders and all the other personality traits that go with each individual. Recognition is established in the normal eye long before the face is near enough to be examined, so that the face is used merely for verification. Teach your eyes to follow this procedure.

Drill for Facial Recognition

Get the family to play "picture stars." Have each one register an emotion and see if you can discover what emotion they are trying to depict. Do this by shifting the gaze rapidly all over the face.

Another Drill: When you sit in an audience facing a platform, or in a church facing a choir, shift from face to face opposite you, analyzing the slight differences of countenance.

Study the bodily traits of picture stars on the screen, then study the faces—the close-ups. Motion pictures are a great aid in recognition of faces, because the portrait is so enlarged and remains in view for analysis longer than flesh and blood expressions.

You will find that going to the motion pictures can aid in building your vision.

IX

TROUBLE IN READING

Does the print blur when you read? Or isn't your arm long enough? If you have worn bi-focals for many years you may need the help of an experienced Bates instructor to enable you once more to read easily at a normal distance. This should be done readily, even though without your glasses you cannot read a word of print at any distance. But you will need help.

If, however, your strain in reading is of short duration, you should improve your reading vision yourself by these relaxation principles by re-educating your eyes to accommodate at normal distances. First of all, practice for several weeks the relaxation suggestions given in the early part of this book. Of these, the most important are the sun bathing, the palming and the swings—getting the feel of the world in motion about you, an illusion difficult to the presbyopic eye (see footnote, page 66).

Vision is a matter of contrast. Eyes do their seeing by comparing largeness and smallness, lightness and darkness, nearness and farness, curves and straightness. These principles can be utilized in teaching the eye to read. For this we use fine print, such as the microscopic type reproduced on page 65. Seat yourself in the best light obtainable, preferably bright sunshine. Remove your glasses, palm your eyes, then dip the closed eyelids in the light or sun; now you are ready to work with the print.

Hold the page at arm's length, resting your eyes gently on what you know to be white spaces between the lines, blinking continuously and breathing easily. Then bring it a little closer and continue, always resting the eyes on the spaces between the print rather than on the lines themselves. By degrees the spaces will clear and become more vivid, not only at arm's length but when you get the print quite close to your eyes. It is never an effort to look at a blank space. If someone puts marks on that space the interpretation of those marks may require effort. If we could coax our eyes to stay more on the white spaces between the print than on the printed mark, we would be able to read vividly and speedily, because we would do away with effort.

When the eyes have relaxed on the fine print so that you can see clear white spaces at reading distance, take a book with good print, hold it in the sun, and pretending that your eyes are paint brushes, paint white under the rows of printing from margin to margin of the page, moving your head to help the eyes paint along. See the print begin to clear. If not, put sun or light on your eyes again. Palm them; bathe them in light once more and play with the fine print again. Then return to the book print. Gradually, the eyes should catch on and learn to slide along on the white—*"streamline reading."*

When the print begins to flash out and you are able to read along, do not continue your reading until the eyes are exhausted and the vision fades. Anticipate the point of weariness by closing your eyes on the period of each good-sized sentence. If you rest before you are tired, the eyes will not become exhausted. By closing, I mean let the lids cover the eyes gently—gently, not tight!—and remain closed until the eyes feel loose and easy. Then take a big breath; think of the last word you did see. Open the eyes and they will return like little homing pigeons to that word. Stroke white under the word until it clears. Then you can continue reading with comfort. The presbyopic (see footnote, p. 66) eye often takes a moment to clear on opening. Do this clearing on the last word you saw. The mental picture of the last word seen and the return to it when you open are important points in restoring vision to eyes that have difficulty in reading without glasses.

Here is another drill, using the microscopic type—the "large-to-small-print" drill. When, without glasses, your reading vision has improved for normal print, sit in the sun and play with the two specimens of type on pages 64 and 65, copies of the same article, "The Mental Side of Seeing." Prepare your eyes for close work by sunning, palming, and sunning again on the closed lids. During this entire drill, keep the head moving gently from side to side in a short swing.

Now, sitting lazily with your back to the sun, and the two pages in the sun, stroke white spaces from margin to margin between the lines of large print, then do the same between the lines of microscopic print. Don't try to read or make out words. At first, put your thumbnail under the title of the small print. Read the title of the large print, then say the words from memory as you look over your thumbnail at the white space under the tiny title. Close eyes, rest, breathe and swing your head. Repeat three or four times. Don't mind if the tiny words do not come out. You are just playing with it anyway, not trying to read. Be careful to keep your eyes loosely, easily open—no squinching!

Next, slide under the first four words of the paragraph in large type, then slide with the thumbnail and vision under the first four words of the tiny print, just easily. After several times of this, the word-lengths will space off correctly, even though you can't yet read the words. Sun the closed eyes and play with the rest of the top line, large size, then say and remember the words for the small size. Continue, line after line, a few words at a time.

Don't work too long at a sitting—rather, try it again another sunny day. Some day the words will flash out from the microscopic print, and eventually you will relax your eyes to the degree that you can read them. The purpose in learning to read micro print is to develop the maximum in reading relaxation. It is impossible to read micro print if you strain or make effort or try. The words clear only when the eyes are thoroughly relaxed. When the eyes relax to this point, every nerve in the body loosens.

For years we have been taught that sun on the page is injurious to the eye. In reality, the better the light the easier it is to read. Sun is the best light. If you doubt this, compare the ease of reading on a sunny day with the increased effort on a dark or cloudy day. Sunshine on the page brings out the sharpest contrast of black and white to aid the eye in reading. Many eyes with dim vision or clouded by cataract can be taught to read fine print with sun on the page.

Of course, no one can read comfortably in a glare. By tipping the page about experimentally in the sunlight you can find an angle at which there is no glare and still have the brightest sun on the page.

Again review the chapter about preparing the eyes to accept sunshine comfortably by dipping the closed lids in sun.

Warning: Avoid trick vision—squeezing the lids into a slit or holding them in any other set or special way to clear*

* Text continues on p. 66.

The Mental Side of Seeing

The most wonderful results in vision building come from understanding the mental side of seeing, for strange as it may sound, vision is only one-tenth physical and nine-tenths mental. Since this is true, activities of the mind under relaxed conditions can be made to accomplish wonderful things for the eyes.

Eyes that obtain improved sight on the letters by aid of the memory and imagination very soon obtain improved vision for everything, for memory and imagination improve near-sight, far-sight, astigmatism, cataract, and many more serious diseases of the eye formerly considered incurable.

To understand how this can occur, we can demonstrate that imperfect sight is produced by an effort. You are eager to see the word or letter so you look "hard" and it blurs. Then you close your eyes, remember the blur and wonder what the letters might have been. Now, memory of imperfect sight brings still more imperfect sight, producing a higher degree of refractive error. You can prove to yourself that it is this mental strain that lowers the vision, the strain being in the mind, not locally in the eye itself. In all cases of imperfect sight, a mental strain can first be recognized—a mental effort or confusion. The moment this strain is relaxed the vision improves—without exception!

It is very important that the mental activity be understood because—and this is a law—imperfect sight is not possible without first a mental strain.

Now there are many ways of getting rid of this strain and securing the relaxation that brings vision. The best way of all is the simplest—by memory! Clear visual memory of anything is beneficial. To remember a house or a chair is a great help, but one obtains still greater assistance by the memory of a very small part of a house or a chair—the door-knob or the top of the chair-back, for the smaller the object the more perfectly it can be remembered or imagined or seen.

The moment a person becomes convinced that he is suffering from a mental strain as well as an eyestrain, progress toward a complete recovery in a very short time is obtained.

—Condensed from articles
by W. H. Bates, M.D.

MICROSCOPIC TYPE

The Mental Side of Seeing

The most wonderful results in vision batfling come from understanding the mental side of seeing, for strange as it may sound, vision is only one-tenth physical and nine-tenths mental. Since this is true, activities of the mind under relaxed conditions can be made to accomplish wonderful things for the eyes.

Eyes that obtain improved sight on the letters by aid of the memory and imagination very soon obtain improved vision for everything, for memory and imagination improve near sight, far sight, astigmatism, cataract, and many more serious diseases of the eye formerly considered incurable.

To understand how this can occur, we can demonstrate that imperfect sight is produced by an effort. You are eager to see the word or letter so you look "hard" and it falters. Then you close your eyes, remember the blur and wonder what the letters might have been. Now, memory of imperfect sight brings still more imperfect sight, producing a higher degree of refractive error. You can prove to yourself that it is this mental strain that lowers the vision, the strain being in the mind, not locally in the eye itself. In all cases of imperfect sight, a mental strain can first be recognized—a mental effort or tension. The moment this strain is relaxed the vision improves—without exception!

It is very important that the mental activity be understood because—and this is a law—imperfect sight is not possible without first a mental strain.

Now there are many ways of getting rid of this strain and securing the relaxation that brings vision. The best way of all is the simplest—by memory! Clear visual memory of anything is beneficial. To remember a house or a chair is a great help, but one obtains still greater assistance by the memory of a very small part of a house or a chair—the door-knob or the top of the chair-back, for the smaller the object the more perfectly it can be remembered or imagined or seen.

The moment a person becomes convinced that he is suffering from a mental strain as well as an eyestrain, progress toward a complete recovery in a very short time is obtained.
—Condensed from articles
by W. H. Bates, M.D.

the print. Far from aiding the attainment of normal vision, this actually increases the strain. Beginners in eye training often discover that by lowering the upper lid, or peeking through the lashes of the tightened eyelids, the print suddenly clears up and can be read vividly. This is not true vision but artificial accommodation, and lowers the power of the eye, because it is an effort. Don't "squinch"!

If, after repeated trials, repeated quiet relaxation periods with this fine print in the sun, you do not get results, find a good instructor of the Bates Method. He or she will be able readily to show you other more involved drills to release the vision latent in all eyes so long as the optic nerve is alive. Remember, vision is like water in a faucet; relaxation turns it on; tension turns it off. You can prove this to yourself.

All the previous relaxation drills should help turn on this wonderful vision. Any drill you give yourself that coaxes the eye to change quickly from the distant point to the near point is an advantage. The calendar drill mentioned before can be made valuable for presbyopic and hypermetropic* eyes by looking at the number on the calendar each time before look-ing at the number on the watch face. At first, the calendar may be clear and the face of the watch blurred, no number

---

* By presbyopic eye, we mean the eye that is held permanently flat by the four recti muscles, hence is kept focused for the distance when it should be allowed to lengthen if you wish to do close work. People notice this condition when they find they must hold their print increasingly further from their eyes. It is miscalled "old age sight"; it can come on at any age, and will leave when the eye learns to lengthen for close work. Hypermetropic, or far-sighted eyes, have always preferred to stay flat and look far, even though some people may be able to force the eyeballs to lengthen at times, but with effort, strain or pain. In both presbyopic and hypermetropic conditions, the four flattening muscles can be loosened by relaxation, thus allowing the two obliques to come into play.

legible. But if you breathe deeply and keep looking easily from the figure one on the calendar to the figure one on your watch, closing the eyes to rest; then from the two on the calendar to the two on your watch, and close; from the three on the calendar to the three on your watch—by the time you reach twelve you may see the number on your watch. But look *easily. Rest. And breathe!*

The domino drill, previously described, can be made most valuable by sitting closer and closer as the eyes improve.

At the movies, try to go without your glasses. When people with bifocals or glasses for far-sighted eyes first view motion pictures without their spectacles, they may have to sit either closer to or farther from the screen than the glasses allowed. Locate the distance from the screen at which the eyes feel most comfortable and see with the least effort. Rest the eyes easily on the screen. At first, the picture will be blurred; but if you breathe deeply and keep shifting your gaze from one portion of the picture to the other, blinking often, your eyes will soon adjust themselves. At first, perhaps, you may not be able to stand a whole show without your lenses. Only by easy degrees can the body be weaned from crutches. Palm in the dark between pictures when you can. Be sure and palm when you return home. Eventually, if you are patient, you should be able to view the picture comfortably with the naked eye and sit progressively nearer to or farther from the screen. The normal eye can adapt itself comfortably to the screen from as close as the first row, preferably in the center section. A person with normal eyes should be able to sit anywhere in the theater with equal comfort. Presbyopia (old-age sight) can be forestalled and prevented in all types of eyes, by practicing close vision with relaxation.

X

MUSCLE IMBALANCE

Working with subnormal eyes in our studio we find that muscle imbalance, even though slight, can be held responsible for much poor vision and great discomfort, often even headaches and nausea. Hence, in building vision, we pay attention to the slightest tendency of an eye to slip off focus.

The possessor of eyes with muscular imbalance often needs help in determining which eye tends slightly in or slightly out. A friend or member of the family may be called upon to decide. Sometimes a baby picture will tell the story by giving evidence of a slight cast. Once you determine which direction the eye goes off focus, you will know which way it should be coaxed. That side should be favored in all visual activity.

Suppose the left eye tends slightly in. The book you read should be held in the left hand to coax the vision out to the left. At church or theater sit on the right of the auditorium, if possible. If not, twist slightly in your chair so that the vision must be toward the left.

If the eyes are really crossed (either in or out) —that is, if you suffer from what the doctors call strabismus or squint— you will not be able to do these muscle drills until you have had help from a Bates instructor in getting the eyes somewhat into alignment and the eye with weaker vision strengthened in visual acuity. But if your eyes are only slightly off focus (and few people have perfect focus) there is a drill which may bring them into complete alignment, relaxing pulled muscles and tense nerves. This drill may be practiced many times a day with no ill effects, as it eases rather than tires the eyes. It is a relaxation, not an exercise.

Double Image Drill

Remove glasses; then palm the eyes, or close them gently and breathe deeply until relaxed. Now, making sure that the head is not tipped to one side or the other, hold a pencil at arm's length, pointing the eraser at your nose. Bring the pencil gently toward your nose, blinking all the time. When it reaches a distance of three inches from your nose hold the pencil up vertically and let your vision travel rapidly up and down the pencil from eraser to point three or four times, then look quickly away, at a distant wall or space past the eraser. The tip of the pencil will separate into two pencils, close together, perhaps, at first. Close your eyes, loosen everything, and in your mind's eye place the pencil tips half an inch wider apart than you saw them. Open and again look relaxedly at the wall, and the tips will be wider. Close again and repeat until the pencils seem to be three inches apart. Now, as you continue to look easily at the wall, move your head slightly from side to side; the two pencils move but keep their distance from each other. If this is done correctly it removes all effort or sense of tension from the interior of the eyes and from the surrounding muscles.

Caution: Do every step of this drill easily: blink gently and keep the eyes loose, and the look-away gentle—not a hard stare.

Two-Finger Drill for Focus

Remove glasses. Hold the forefingers of both hands up in front of you a foot from your nose, your hands about two feet from each other. Start your head swinging gently from side to side. Rest your visual attention on the left finger tip, then on the right, then on the left, then on the right. Close your eyes, keeping up the swing and thinking from one finger to the other as though looking through closed lids. Now, bring the fingers a few inches closer to each other, open the eyes and continue, seeing one finger best, then the other finger best— four times, shifting your vision from the one finger to the other without blinking. Close, continuing the swing, and move the fingers a few inches closer (now about eight inches apart). When the fingers were the widest distance apart it was easy to leave the one and go to the other. As they approach another closer and closer it will be harder to make the complete shift from one finger to the other. Of course, as the fingers near each other you will not entirely lose consciousness of the finger you are not looking at, but you will see more vividly the finger that holds your visual and mental focus. Keep moving them point by point closer until finally the fingers touch. Then see if you can successfully shift from one fingernail to the other, leaving behind the one and seeing more vividly the other. This is particularly good for eyes with a muscle imbalance; and for eyes with dim vision there may be a flash of clarity at the end of the drill.

I once worked in our studio with a lad who had been blinded by a serious eye condition and had only light perception. We were gradually strengthening his eyes and building up the vision, but he had never yet seen more than one object in a glance. One day as he sat in an automobile he practiced this drill of shifting from one finger to the other—seeing one finger best, then the other. When he finished the drill he lifted his gaze and looked out the car window, and got a flash of vision that took his breath away. For the first time since his baby days he saw vividly green grass, white house, blue sky and sidewalks.

The domino and calendar work, earlier described, can all be used to good advantage, favoring the eye that needs coaxing into alignment.

In these drills watch the tilt of your head. Do not let it tip to one side or the other, but keep it erect over the spinal column so you could shake your head, "No, no," or nod your head, "Yes, yes," with equal facility.

There are many swings and drills used in our methods to straighten crossed eyes which would also be good for muscle imbalance, and which would make a lesson or two from a skilled Bates instructor worth while.

Eyes with muscle imbalance are sprained eyes, just as a sprained ankle creates off balance in a foot. It takes time to rectify a sprain—time and daily attention until normalcy has been restored.

XI

INSOMNIA

If you suffer from eye strain and nerves you probably need to learn how to fall asleep, for eye strain and insomnia often go together.

First of all, a warm drink before bedtime draws the blood from the head and gives a sense of comfort to the inner being.

Then, a number of deep easy breaths before an opened window supplies the oxygen needed in the blood.

The long swing done one hundred times, which takes a mere two minutes, gives the spine a soothing massage and tires the muscles enough to make them want to lie down.

Next, teach the body by an example of sharp contrast what real tension is, so it may learn the other extreme, complete relaxation. Do this by holding the body rigid while you count ten, tightening every atom of your being from the roots of your hair to the soles of your feet. When you permit yourself to let go, the loosening will be equally complete because every nerve and muscle will be glad to be relieved. This can be repeated several times until you know what it feels like to lie limp.

Next, stretch and yawn several times to the full extent of your reach in different directions. Do the same with your limbs. This is different from the tensing above, as it is done loosely and easily. While you are stretching, yawn thoroughly with as deep a breath as you can summon. Many people yawn with their teeth clenched or their mouths only partly open. Teach yourself what the full yawn is like. Drop your chin on your chest. Take your head away back and leave your chin behind as you inhale. Come back and get your chin as you exhale. Indulge in this several times.

Now, as you lie limply in bed, palm. Crowd an extra pillow under your elbows as a brace if you palm flat on your back. Or, if you lie on your side, only one elbow needs a prop.

So far these directions have pertained to the body, but it may be the mind that is keeping you awake. Memory brings relaxation—memory of something that you have looked at and enjoyed seeing. Counting sheep may fail us here, for few people, these days, have actually stood at a gate and counted sheep. Hence this practice would be in the nature of writing a composition or composing a picture which would take some effort, and would keep us awake. But we have all actually seen the letters of our alphabet. Most of us have stood before a blackboard, so if we do the blackboard drill described in the chapter on palming, real relaxation will result. If you tire of the blackboard, any of the mental swings previously explained may put you to sleep.

Add to the above the fact taught us by different neurologists—that the body will take all the sleep it needs, and is resting and repairing itself so long as you lie quietly even though sleep does not come; then the fear of insomnia will be relieved and sleep is more liable to overtake you. Thrashing from side to side, not lack of sleep, is what makes a person exhausted after a night of insomnia.

Mental swings, and pleasant mental picture memories of happy days, are a good substitute for thrashing. You will be sound asleep long before you have exhausted the list.

XII

EMOTIONAL EYE STRAIN

Emotions cause eye strain and, contrariwise, eye strain causes emotions.

Anyone under the devastating influence of grief, blighting disappointment or distracting worry, is under such nerve strain that his eyes are seriously affected—only temporarily perhaps; but if he does not know how to treat them, the strain may become permanent and do lasting damage. Such eyes are sick eyes and should be treated with a consideration accorded a sick person, until the emotional misery has modified or passed.

On the other hand, anyone under the nerve-wracking influence of strained eyes is subject to harassing emotions that obsess him whether he gives vent to them or not—irritability and short answers that come, not from the heart, but from nerves raw beyond endurance. Or, if he be the controlled type, the irritability may be repressed and take the form of resentful moodiness, indigo depressions or black forebodings.

We all know that emotional stress and shock affect the body. The heart skips a beat; the stomach turns over. "When I heard that news I turned deathly sick" or "That telegram made me positively ill!" are common exclamations. Excitement or great joy will do the same thing. The rush to get off on a pleasure trip robs us of appetite for breakfast; we just

74

"don't feel hungry." A fit of anger will produce heartburn or acute indigestion. People in grief and sorrow should not, and usually cannot, eat.

What is thus generally known about the stomach is seldom recognized about the eyes, yet eyes are an even more accurate barometer of the emotions. "He turned blind with rage." "He saw red with anger." "His joy was so great the world swam before his eyes." Such phrases are not just rhetorical flights but actual happenings. The mental strain is so great that it reacts on the eyes, temporarily interfering with vision. This is the reason each witness of a terrible accident gives a different account. The moment of shock-blindness comes at a different instant to each pair of eyes, hence each person actually sees a different accident.

A young lady who had just finished normalizing her near-sighted eyes was giving them a final workout at the studio. She was reading small sentences with ease from the end of the long studio. Suddenly she put her hand to her head; her face distorted with pain and she said, "I can't see it!" Immediate investigation disclosed that while letting her eyes do their work, she had been mentally distracted by trying to plan how she could possibly get forty necessary tasks accomplished before her train left in the morning. The instructor had her sit down, list the forty things, organize them as to their importance, relationship and the possibility of fitting them into the remaining time. The very listing and organizing relieved the girl's distracted mind; the pain left and she was able to finish her final lesson with good vision and perfect comfort.

As Doctor Bates has said, "There is no such thing as eye strain without first a mental strain or confusion."

After a lovers' quarrel a young lady drove her car headlong

into a rock crusher on the street. So blinding were her emotions that she did not see it.

It is important to understand this about the eyes in order to know how to treat them under the emotional tension to which all mortals are subject. After a sleepless night of grief or worry you would not think of eating a heavy meal in the morning. The very thought would be revolting, and if we do eat anything it is liable to lie undigested in the stomach for hours. Yet, under these same conditions we will go to the office and put the eyes through a heavy day's routine of close work in artificial light, then wonder why the eyes rebel with pain, headache, dim or blurred vision and muscle pullings. "My glasses don't seem to be strong enough," you will complain, or "My eyes are giving me fits; I'll have to get stronger lenses." What is really needed is a little mental and emotional calm. If that is not possible, get some outdoor exercise to soothe both spirit and nerves and do some or all of the relaxing swings and mental drills; then, as the nerves and mind regain composure, the poor eyes will have a chance to relax and regain their normalcy.

Two business partners arguing heatedly over a policy to be pursued became so angry that neither could read the document before them. One said the whole thing looked like a series of "Q's." The other complained that the printers had used such poor ink that the words ran together. Wisely, they gave up straining to see and called the secretary, who read the print easily and clearly with no complaints. She did not share their emotional strain.

The damage that tension can do to eyes is frequently demonstrated in the so-called "Kleig eyes" of those engaged in the motion picture industry. Kleig eyes used to be a very chemical thing. The minute particles of carbon from the old Kleig lights permeated the air and actually entered and poisoned the actor's eyes. Now that the lights are improved, Kleig eyes come from intense mental strain and stress in the production of emotions on demand—emotions that are not actually felt. This tension shuts off the circulation from the eyes, which consequently suffer. The lights get the blame. If professional people understood how to take the sun, which is the brightest light, to make eyes and the retinal nerves immune to brilliance, the brightness of the lights would relieve rather than bother the eyes when under strain. If they knew how to relax their eyes and nerves between scenes and during rest periods they would suffer no inconvenience from the Kleigs. Tension is the cause of the trouble, not the brightness. Eyes are built for light. They thrive on it.

A bookkeeper in a large office was falsely accused of making a serious mistake, and was called on the carpet by her superior. Because of office politics she had to accept the blame and was punished accordingly. Until this incident occurred, her eyes, under our instruction, were rapidly approaching normalcy, though for years previously she had worn glasses. This office tragedy in her career gave the eyes a terrific setback, with pain and lowered vision, until the cause was uncovered—emotional strain. We analyzed the situation, giving her a different viewpoint of the incident and proving to her how merely temporary a catastrophe it was—a thing she would not be able to remember in a few years' time. This changed her emotional reaction. At once the eye strain was relieved, the pain ceased and good vision returned.

Strong emotions can even result in blindness.

Eye Strain Causing Temperament

Most people realize that when they "fly off the handle" the temper comes not from their hearts but is due to strained nerves irritated one degree too far. Even babies have these temperamental outbursts, and for the same reason—the nerve strain often being caused by some bad strain in the eyes. Cross-eyed babies are quite given to tantrums, and when they attain school age are often called problem children, later perhaps being considered incorrigible. This temperament is due solely to the pulled and straining eye muscles and the attempt to see with the wrong part of the retina, the false macula, which is not adequate for keen seeing. Once the tension in these muscles is loosened so that the eyes can swing into alignment and the true center of sight trained to do the seeing, these children become sweet lovable characters. Most of them become unusually good students as a reaction when released from the terrible tension that heretofore had held them back.

In conclusion, it is far easier to relieve the eye strain and restore the emotions to their healthy balance than it is to aid once normal eyes to weather distracting worry, overpowering disappointment or lasting sorrow.

XIII

RECREATION

Motion Pictures

Contrary to popular belief and teaching, motion pictures are good for the eyes. If you know how to view them you can reduce the degree of your refractive error. The subnormal eye by tension holds down the active seventy-time-a-second shifting necessary to normalcy. Now, the motion picture shifts forty-eight times a second. To see it at all the subnormal eye must increase its speed. The moment this happens some of the tension is reduced and the eye becomes more nearly normal.

"But pictures hurt my eyes; I just don't go to the movies," one often hears. Not the picture but the wrong method of looking at them is what does the damage. If the eye tries by a stare to hold this swift-moving film still, pain and discomfort are the result. If, however, one relaxes in his seat, breathes deeply, gets his head at a comfortable position, held high enough so that the nose points toward the screen and the eyes can indulge in a downward focus, then the picture can be observed in comfort and relaxation, with vision actually improving as the film goes on. Learn to let your eye travel all over the screen instead of keeping it fixed on one spot. Glance occasionally into the black darkness for an instant of rest. If you wish to watch the star's expression as she emotes, shift your attention all over her face from eyes to mouth, to chin, to hairline, rather than fasten on the face as a whole. Or glance quickly from her face to the one she is talking to and back again; in short, prevent a stare.

In the emotional excitement of the story, check on yourself. Are you holding your breath? If you are, your eyes are robbed of their normal circulation and oxygen and they will suffer. So breathe deeply; blink often and let your eyes roam.

Near-sighted people should sit quite close to the screen at first, in the second or third row, to see without their glasses; and increase the distance from month to month as the vision improves. Far-sighted people should sit where it is most comfortable to see without glasses, and shorten the distance as the eyes improve.

Recognition of faces is the greatest difficulty for people with poor distant-vision. The movies are a great aid in this. To begin with, an enlarged picture of the face is presented so that slight variations in expression are magnified and can be registered by the dim or sluggish eye; whereas in the real countenance, expressions are so slight and transitory that they escape imperfect eyes entirely. Again, the picture in close-ups allows more time for the audience to study facial expression which the real face never gives.

The motion picture has spoiled us for plays on the legitimate stage. Before the advent of movies we never expected to see clearly the star's face on the stage without the aid of opera glasses. Now we are so used to watching faces and expressions in detail on the screen that the eye at the theater unconsciously strains to see the actor's face as vividly as faces on the screen. The result is that many people, these days, strain their eyes greatly at the theater or the opera, attempting to do the impossible.

Television

Many inquiries come to us about television. Is television bad for the eyes? Why do eyes sting and burn after viewing television? What can be done to make eyes more comfortable while viewing television?

We believe that watching the screen of a good television set is as advantageous in vision-building as watching motion pictures. However, care should be taken that best conditions should prevail.

There should be plenty of fresh air in the room. Eyes must have oxygen. Often windows and doors of a living room will be sealed while the family, literally breathless, watches the performance.

Each person should sit at his or her most favorable distance, a distance at which there is no effort to see. As nearly as possible each one should sit in front of the screen rather than at the side, which would give a slanting view.

Good posture should be maintained, sitting erect with the head well balanced over the spinal column. Many people, especially children, tend to lean forward with chin thrust out, which interferes with the circulation as well as the angle of vision. So often people recline, and lying on one side watch the screen, thus pulling the eyes completely out of alignment. I know one family in which the children are tucked into bed to lie and watch the television far across the room until they fall asleep. The parents are amazed that the strained eyes and nerves bring irritability and tantrums the next day.

Television authorities advise light in the room because the small screen needs additional light. Extra light prevents the picture from being the only bright spot in the total darkness.

Rest the eyes occasionally. Too protracted looking in one direction at one spot is very fatiguing. Frequently, the television viewer should give several quick looks off into the room. Or better yet, during a lull in the screen's activities, the eyes should be given the complete rest of palming for a moment or two. Covering the closed eyes with the warm palms, even for the count of forty, will save you much eye strain. Frequent blinking is also a great rest for the eyes. I have seen television viewers with eyes glued to the screen as if boring holes with their vision.

In conclusion, television can be good for the eyes. If the above directions are carefully followed, eyes with short vision may be able, as the weeks pass by, to sit increasingly far from the screen. Conversely, far-sighted eyes may find it possible to edge comfortably a bit closer, with noticeable and increasing clarity of vision. One pupil, who once suffered during long evenings before the television set, now knits under good light, looking back and forth from her hand work to the screen. Unlimited viewing in this manner brings no strain, discomfort or fatigue.

Play

Take time out to play—some each day. Play games. If you do not know any, learn some. For sedentary workers there are big muscle games: any ball game, fast walks, horseshoes, handball, skating, ping pong, dancing, bowling, tennis. And for those with tired muscles, mental games: cards, anagrams, crossword puzzles, jackstraws, building match towers on bottle tops. Avoid games that might encourage staring (checkers and chess), or mental strain (difficult jigsaw puzzles).

Doctor Bates teaches us that one reason for the increasing prevalence of eye strain today is the fact that we have lost the art and spirit of play. If we take up golf, we hire a professional and make a business of it. If we attempt tennis, we engage a coach and work as hard at our play as we did at our daily task. We play bridge with a dagger at our belts, indulging in as much mental strain as would be required in a business deal. We no longer enjoy carefree, laughing play just for the fun of it. But we can relearn. Anyone will find it quite amusing to play handball against the wall all by himself occasionally. Simple as this is, it relaxes the nerves and loosens the eyes. Playing, or even watching, ping-pong, tennis or bowling gives the eyes opportunity for happy shifting. Dancing is also good. If you have not time to dance formally, do a few steps to the radio in solitude each evening. Again the eyes and nerves respond, for in dancing more than in any other activity we let the world go by.

People with defective vision or eye strain frequently admit that they never have played even in childhood. If such individuals can be coaxed to get into the spirit of a carefree, happy game, it brings them a relaxation they may never have known before. At first, so simple a thing as throwing a ball up and catching it may be difficult for such a person, because mind and muscles have never been trained to co-ordinate.

One man could not catch a ball that he had thrown into the air two feet. The ball returned to his hand but fell on a flat and unresponsive palm, fingers failing to close. When this co-ordination is learned, it brings with it relaxation that permeates the entire nervous system.

Motoring Points

Do your eyes tire when driving or, worse yet, when riding as a passenger? Probably you stare straight ahead out the windshield, fastening your gaze on the straightaway, staring at the point of vanishment. Probably also your head is ducked and you are looking up under furrowed brows, squeezing the lids tensely against the brightness.

To avoid eye strain while motoring, practice the following simple rules:

Bathe your closed lids in sun before entering the car, or, if at night, dip your closed eyes in the brightness of the headlights.

Keep your head erect above your spine and look where your nose is pointing.

Then, instead of fastening your gaze on the highway, keep shifting your attention ahead from one side of the straightaway to the other, remembering to blink, frequently glancing at the instrument board or windshield wiper and away again. Briefly, do not hold your eyes in a set, fixed position ahead. The roving eye sees everything; the eye that is fixed in one direction is startled by a passing car. A very good drill to teach the eyes a quick change from near to far is to glance at a numeral on your watch face, then sweep the horizon with your vision. This makes the eyeball lengthen quickly at the near point and flatten quickly as you focus at the distance, which keeps it supple. Again—the camera principle.

XIV

MENTAL VISION

Psychologists admit that vision is truly mental. Nine-tenths of seeing is done in the brain, only one-tenth in the eye itself. For this reason, working with the eye alone takes care of the least of the trouble when there is defective vision. Allotting so much to the brain may seem extreme, yet we have all had the experience of reading several pages with our minds far removed, and suddenly awakening to the fact that we did not know a thing we had read. Although the eyes, like little cameras, had registered the series of pictures accurately enough, the mind had failed to interpret them.

That is why boredom causes eye strain. The mind, losing interest, gives but slight attention, thus leaving the eyes to struggle along with only partial co-operation. The disinterested mind attempts apathetically to do two things at one time, which is impossible. Since there is no such thing as eye strain without first a mental strain, a strained, bored mind registers immediately in lowered vision.

Eye strain is often developed in school children when the novelty of school days has worn off and they are bored by required subjects for which they have neither aptitude nor interest. This eye strain may easily become permanent and may increase as the years go by.

Mental strain often damages the eyes even though they remain closed. A gentleman with severe eye strain once came to the studio. He had been utilizing a two-hour daily train trip to practice a course in memory training. The prescribed rules of this course were mechanical and monotonous, but he did them with great determination, keeping his eyes closed in supposed rest while he concentrated. Each morning he arrived at his desk with eyes so strained he could scarcely use them— more tired than after a whole day's work. We proved to him that the eyes had suffered because of the mental tension he was inducing by the unnatural concentration he forced upon himself.

Familiar Versus Unfamiliar Objects

Memory and imagination are the means by which the mind necessarily interprets the image registered on the sensitive plate, the retina. Were it not for these two mental processes we would look at an object and say, "I see something but I cannot make it out."

For instance, if you were to meet a golliwog, there being no such thing, the eye and mind would both be baffled. You would reach into your experienced memory and say, "It looks like a——," and by imagination you would try that something on the golliwog, but the eye, being truthful, would cancel the comparison as false, and you would think, "No, it cannot be that; perhaps it is——." Again you would reach into memory and by imagination try to fit on shapes from past experience, until finally, having nothing from the past to aid in the interpretation of the golliwog, you would give up and say, "Well, something is there but I just cannot make it out." In other words, without memory and imagination, intelligible vision cannot take place.

A group of motorists, each with good vision, demonstrated vividly how memory interpreted by imagination controls sight. Their attention was attracted to something in the air far ahead. One member of the party with desert-trained eyes looked at the object in the sky and declared, "It is an eagle high over the valley." Another member said, "No, it isn't over the valley; it is an airplane far off over the mountains." Another said, "That isn't far away at all. It is a little hawk hovering over its prey in the meadow close to the highway." The argument continued, each firm in his interpretation of the vision, by his own memory experience imagining the thing to be what he knew best. Finally the automobile came within a few yards of the object, which turned out to be a glider kite attached to a long string in the hands of a man. The remarkable fact about this incident is that these people had normal vision, yet each held his own opinon based on his personal experience, until the party was close enough to see the string attached to the kite.

Familiar objects are seen easily; unfamiliar objects, with difficulty. The necessity for mental interpretation of anything the eye observes is the reason that unfamiliar objects are so hard to see; sometimes it requires such effort that frequently refractive error is produced, even in the normal eye. It was discovered that school children with normal vision usually develop refractive error when first regarding a strange map. It is the task of interpreting the many strange items in a museum or exposition that fags the brain, reacts on the eye and exhausts a person in a short while. The mind and eyes at the office or factory can attend many more things, do much more actual seeing for a longer period of time without fatigue, because there they see familiar objects which involve no mental tax or strain. Factory workers put in eight hours a day of detailed precision work and are quick to detect the slightest flaw in the product that passes through their hands. Yet these same workers would become exhausted by a one-hour period of inspecting unfamiliar exhibits in a museum.

Memory Brings Vision

Since normal vision is not possible without perfect memory and imagination, you can see only what you remember and imagine. Contrariwise, we often bring vision to dimming eyes, and turn vision on from a perfect mind through imperfect eyes, by memory and imagination, because if you can remember and imagine a thing, you can then hope to see it. Objects that dimming eyes have seen and can remember have a chance to be seen again because memory brings vision.

Eyes with dim vision, renewing their mental picture of an object by the sense of touch, may soon be able "to make it out" visually, and later may develop a real sense of seeing it.

Again, if a strange object cannot be seen, the clear mental picture of any object that has been seen perfectly, and can be remembered vividly, brings sufficient relaxation to the eyes to permit vision for the strange object.

Relaxation is easily brought about by a perfect mental picture of anything one can bring to memory, whether foreign or related to the object desired to be seen. If you can close the eyes and visualize perfectly how your own name would look in print, you can see the objects before you if you can retain that mental picture with your eyes open. Until re-educated, dim eyes cannot get or hold a mental picture.

Unconscious Vision

A large part of our vision is unconscious. While we know this to be true, we seldom give it attention.

Suppose you were walking down a crowded city sidewalk on the way to your office. You are talking over an important financial problem with a friend, looking earnestly into his eyes, driving home every point and studying his reactions. Yet during this heated argument you are threading your way through the crowd, sidestepping someone who would bump you, stopping at the curb when the signal changed, stepping off with the *Go* sign, and finally turning into the office building and pressing the elevator bell. Never once did you consciously look around. This was all automatic action, you believe. True, but you were guided by unconscious vision, real vision despite the fact that it was not conscious on your part, your conscious vision having been on your friend's face. Had the street and building been in black darkness none of this would have been possible.

Since normal eyes use unconscious vision instinctively, sub-normal eyes can have their vision increased by teaching them to take advantage of subconscious vision which is easier to develop, and dimming eyes can be taught once more to see. To be sure, this type of vision lacks minute detail and does not know the satisfaction of having seen unless the mind has registered each detail. But the eye that becomes conscious of light perception and shadowy images is never at ease until the mind back of the eye is satisfied that a visual record has been made, and the identity of the images or shadows determined. Conscious vision can therefore be built on a foundation of unconscious vision.

Only when the eye and mind work in unison can we have a truly satisfactory sense of sight. Since vision is nine-tenths mental, brighten the mind and you will brighten the eyes. The eyes follow the mind, either in a chaos of confusion or in the peace of relaxation.

XV

NORMAL VISION

Three things are necessary for perfect vision: relaxation of the eye during activity, maintenance of the normal shift of the fovea Centralis (seventy times a second), and eye and mind co-ordination.

Normalcy can be possible only when the eye becomes relaxed and maintains this relaxation while at work. Only when the eye is relaxed can the extrinsic muscles function normally: the belting muscles (obliques) contracting for close vision, the flattening muscles (the recti) contracting for distance.

While the seventy times per second shift it taking place, the fovea is able to traverse every atom of the object regarded with such rapidity that it seems as if the object were seen all at once. Only when this speed is maintained does this center of sight, the keenest group of retinal nerves, come into play.

Sight is quicker than thought; the eye is quicker than the mind. Training of eye-mind co-ordination speeds up mind and thought until they are more nearly simultaneous with eye and sight. We have all experienced this speed of vision. If a heavy weight falls suddenly and threatens to mash our toes, we see it, and by reflex action withdraw the foot in time —then get around to thinking, "Heavens! That almost

crushed my foot!" By training, the mind can be speeded until it more nearly approximates the speed of the eye.

When eyes with dim vision first come to the studio and begin training on dominoes, words or letters, the co-ordination of eye and mind is very poor. Often the student will look at a large letter, then with closed eyes wait for perhaps the count of ten before venturing, "Could that have been a T?" In other words, it took several moments for the mind to read and interpret the dim image registered on the retina. As the training continues and the vision improves, this same student becomes increasingly prompt until he can call the letter almost the second the eye meets it. With the perfection of this eye-mind co-ordination all mental processes are stimulated and increased. Since mental efficiency and vision improve together even failing memories can often be restored by improving the vision.

One interesting case we had in the studio was that of an elderly woman suffering from glaucoma whose eyesight and visual memory had failed deplorably. Her memory was so poor that she could look at a double-three domino, read it aloud, close her eyes and then have no idea of what she had just seen. After a second reading she was asked, "What did you see?" "Was it a picture?" she answered. "No, it was a double-three domino," she was told, and was made to look at it and read it aloud again. "Now shut your eyes and tell me, what did you see?" she was asked again. "Was it a letter?" she answered. After the third reading she gave up. "I can't remember what I saw," she replied sadly. In a few weeks of eye training this woman's vision and memory had improved so greatly that she could call the dominoes as fast as she could flash them and remember half a dozen she had just seen.

The most amazing thing about the Bates Method of relaxed vision is the fact that serious conditions of the eye, formerly considered hopeless—such as atrophy, glaucoma, cataract, sympathetic ophthalmia and even detachment and hemorrhage—may often be improved by relaxation, if there is any vision left at all with which to work and if the method is practiced a sufficient length of time.

The Bates Method of vision building is a very deep subject, being truly the psychology of vision. It has been but touched upon in these pages, which offer merely a few workable suggestions to tired, hurting eyes.

People with more obstinate cases of imperfect vision who try to utilize this method would make more rapid progress by obtaining the services of a trained Bates instructor, who would have more and varied devices for the benefit of each individual problem.

Bear in mind that better eyesight—our most valuable possession—is possible to anyone with fair vision. The little time spent daily in improvement and care of the eyes is good insurance against the discomfort, inconvenience and emotional despair of failing vision.